Bently Russell

Books by Beverly Russell

Architecture and Design 1970-1990
New Ideas in America

Women of Design

Forty Under Forty

Women of Taste
Profiles and Recipes of Famous Women Chefs

Six

Design Does Matter

The Adventures of Kundun the Golden Cat
(with Benjamin Beardwood)

Garden Tarot Card Pack
Ask the Flowers

CROSSINGS

Words of Comfort

Edited by

Beverly Russell

CROSSINGS
Words of Comfort

ISBN 978-0-9762905-1-3

Published by Beverly Russell Enterprises
16 School Hill Road
High Falls, NY 12440
www.beverlyrussell.com

Graphic design and layout: Julissa Diaz
Cover design: Julissa Díaz
Design initiative: Adrian Ross
Printing: Lightning Source International

All photographs by Sunday Hendrickson
Except for page 4 Camellia, page 6 Peony, page 14 Iris, page 20 Rose, page 42 Wisteria by Barry Michlin

Library of Congress cataloging in progress

CROSSINGS

Words of Comfort

Edited by

Beverly Russell

Dedicated to:

Elenore Wrench 1900 – 1983

Teacher, comforter, pathfinder
Spiritual Counselor to many during her
remarkable lifetime

"Life must blossom like a flower offering itself to the divine."

The Mother 1878-1973

FOREWORD

Beverly Russell
Elenore Wrench 1900-1983

It was ordained that I should meet Elenore Wrench in the last five years of her life. Just as she had guided people through spiritual counseling in her little white room in the Ritz Tower, then at the corner of 57th Street and Park Avenue, Manhattan, she helped me to another level of consciousness and an understanding of the larger issues of life and death.

Shortly after her 82nd birthday, as she began to experience the physical weakness that was soon to carry her away, we began to consider how her teaching might capture a broader audience, and her influence live on.

While she had numerous letters and documents that were material for a biography, as we considered the selection, it became apparent that less was more. To publish a slim, pocket book of inspirational notes and verses – distillations of favorite writings that she had collected and written over the years – seemed the preferred way of summarizing her remarkable life's work.

These writings reinforce the essential simplicity that Elenore taught was the way to spiritual enlightenment and personal growth: giving thanks, blessing what you have, showing love and being open to receive. She truly believed and had proved again and again, those basic fundamentals are all that you need to accomplish whatever you desire.

CONTENTS

On Metaphysics   page 01
Crocus: *responsible attitude*
Gardenia: *passionate desire*

The Prayer of the Chalice   page 05
Camellia: *independent spirit*

Psalm Ninety One   page 07
Peony: *generous offering*
Tulip: *turning inwards*
Morning Glory: *glorious support*

Spiritual Laws   page 13
Dahlia: *decisive presence*
Iris: *delicate strength*

Follow in his Steps   page 17
Poppy: *remembrance and inspiration*
Anemone: *changing emotions*

Starting a New Year   page 21
Rose: *heady and powerful*

The Way to Your Destiny   page 23
Daffodil: *optimistic determination*

The Way of Life   page 25
Calla Lily: *quiet simplicity*

The Silence   page 27
Freesia: *peacefulness*

One Solitary Life   page 29
Chrysanthemum: *Inspiring leadership*
Cyclamen: *standing tall*

The World is Mine   page 33
Daisy: *worldly innocence*
Sunflower: *forceful impact*

Save Your Strength   page 37
Cosmos: *independent power*
Narcissus: *divine guidance*

Now I am Secure   page 41
Hyacinth: *self assurance*
Wisteria: *enduring friendship*

Slow Me Down   page 45
Sweetpea: *lasting pleasure*
Bougainvillea: *discreet protection*

The Road Not Taken   page 49
Marigold: *sturdy spirit*
Geranium: *joyfulness*

On Metaphysics

A faith in God or gods is common to all
people and this faith is the basis of religion.
We know that some intelligent power rules the
universe and our belief of faith in this power
constitutes our religious convictions.

The laws governing religious conviction are
spiritual and psychological because they
involve our mental or thinking powers.

Mental science is an exact law of mind and
may be understood by anyone who takes the
time properly to study the law of cause and
effect in the mental world.

Metaphysics means "that which goes beyond the known laws of physics." Metaphysics means spiritual philosophy and, from this standpoint, all religious doctrine is metaphysical in its tendency.

Dr. Albert Einstein:
"To understand life, you must step across the thin line that divides physics from metaphysics."

Ralph Waldo Emerson:
"Metaphysics must be perpetually reinforced by life."

Mary Baker Eddy:
"Metaphysics is truth as its highest level."

The Prayer of the Chalice
Frances Nuttall

Father, to you I raise by whole being,
A vessel emptied of self.
Accept, Lord, this my emptiness,
And so fill me with your self
Your light, your love, your life,
That these your precious gifts
May radiate through me and
Overflow the chalice of my heart
Into the hearts of all with whom
I come in contact this day
Revealing to them
The beauty of your joy
And wholeness and the serenity
Of your peace which nothing
Can destroy.

Psalm Ninety One
(modern version)

He that lives in the secret place
Of the most high shall abide under
The shadow of the Almighty.
I will say of the Lord, he is my refuge
And my fortress: My God;
In him will I trust.
Surely he shall deliver me from
The snare of the fowler, and from the
Noisesome pestilence.
He shall cover me with his
Feathers, and under his wings shall
I trust; his truth shall be my shield
And buckler.
I shall not be afraid for the
Terror by night; nor for the arrow that
Flieth by day;

Nor for the pestilence that walks
In darkness; nor for the destruction
That comes at noon.
A thousand shall fall at my side

And ten thousand at my right hand;
But danger shall not come near me.
Only with your eyes shall I
Behold and see the reward of the wicked.
Because Lord, you are my refuge and my
Habitation. No evil shall befall me,
Neither shall any plague come near my
House. For you shall give me angels
Charge over me, to keep me in all your ways.
They shall bear me up in their hands, lest I
Dash my foot against a stone.
I shall tread upon the lion
And adder; but they will not hurt my feet.

Because the Lord has set his love upon me,
Therefore I will survive.
Because he knows my name,
And shall call upon me, and I will
Answer him. He will be with me in trouble;
I will praise him and honor him.
With long life will I acknowledge him
And show my gratitude.

Spiritual Laws
Ralph Waldo Emerson

A little consideration of what takes place
around us every day would show us, that
a higher law than that of our will regulates
events; that our painful labors are
unnecessary, and fruitless; that only in
our easy, simple, spontaneous action are we
strong, and by contenting ourselves with
obedience we become divine. Belief and love, --
a believing love will relieve us of a vast load of
care. O my brothers, God exists. There is a soul
at the centre of nature, and over the will of
every man, so that none of us can wrong the
universe. It has so infused its strong
enchantment into nature, that we prosper
when we accept its advice, and when we
struggle to wound its creatures, our

hands are glued to our sides, or they beat our own breasts.

The whole course of things goes to teach us faith. We need only obey. There is guidance for each of us, and by lowly listening we shall hear the right word. Why need you choose so painfully your place, and occupation, and associates, and modes of action, and of entertainment? Certainly there is a possible right for you that precludes the need of balance and wilful election. For you there is a reality, a fit place and congenial duties.

Place yourself in the middle of the stream of power and wisdom which animates all whom it floats, and you are without effort impelled to truth, to right, and a perfect contentment. Then you put all gainsayers in the wrong. Then you are the world, the measure of right, of truth, of beauty.

Follow in His Steps

The road is too rough, I said.
Dear Lord, there are stones that hurt me so.
And he said,: Dear child I understand,
I walked it long ago.
But there's a cool green path, I said.
Let me walk there for a time.
No child, he gently answered me.
The green road does not climb.
My burden, I said, is far too great.
How can I bear it so?
My child, said he, I remember its weight.
I carried my cross, you know.

But I said, I wish there were friends with me,
Who could make my way their own.
Ah, yes, he said, Gethsemane
Was hard to face alone.

And so I climbed the stony path,
Content at least to know
That where my master had not gone,
I would not need to go.

And strangely then I found new friends
The burden grew less sore
As I remembered, long ago
He went that way before.

Starting a New Year

And I said to the man who stood
At the gate of the year:
Give me a light, that I may tread
Safely into the unknown.
And he replied:
Go on, into the darkness, and put
Your hand into the hand of God.
That shall be to you better than
Light and safer than a known way.
So I went forth and finding the hand
Of God, trod gladly into the night.
And he led me toward the hills and
The breaking of day in the lone East.

The Way to Your Destiny

You think a thought
And you start an action.
You continue the action
And you form a habit.
You follow that habit
And you create a character.
You will your character
And you find your destiny.

The way of Life

I shall pass this way
But once;
Any good thing therefore that
I can do, or any kindness
That I can know,
Let me do it now.
Let me not defer it
Or neglect it.
For I shall not
Pass this way again.

The Silence

Everything you long for
In the silence waits.
Yours the power to shape them
Either, soon or late.
But be very careful
How you form your fate.

One Solitary Life

Here was a young man who was born in an obscure village, the child of a peasant woman. He grew up in another village. He worked in a carpenter shop until he was thirty, and then for three years, he was an itinerant preacher. He never wrote a book. He never held an office. He never owned a home. He never had a family. He never went to college. He never traveled 200 miles from the place he was born. He never did one of the things that usually accompany greatness. He had no credentials but himself.

While he was still a young man, the tide of public opinion turned against him. His friends ran away. He was turned over to his enemies. He went through the mockery of a

trial. He was nailed to a cross between two thieves. While he was dying, his executioners gambled for the only piece of property he had on earth, and that was his coat. When he was dead, he was laid in a borrowed grave through pity of a friend.

Twenty centuries have come and gone and today he is a central figure of the human race and the leader of the column of progress. I am far within the mark when I say that all the armies that ever marched, and all the navies that ever sailed, and all the parliaments that ever sat, and all the kings that ever reigned, put together, have not affected the lives of people upon this earth as has that one solitary life.

The World is Mine

Today, upon a bus, I saw
A lovely maid with golden hair.
I envied her, she seemed so gay,
And I wished I were so fair.
When suddenly she rose to leave,
I saw her hobble down the aisle.
She had one foot, and used a crutch,
But as she passed she had a smile.
Oh, God, forgive me when I whine
I have two feet, the world is mine.

And when I stopped to buy some things
The lad who sold them had such charm.
I talked with him, he said to me:
It's nice to talk to men like you.
You see, he said, I'm blind.
Oh, God, forgive me when I whine
I have two eyes, The world is mine.

Then as I passed along the way,
I saw a child with eyes of blue
He stood and watched the others play.
It seemed he knew not what to do.
I stopped for a moment, and then I said:
Why don't you join the others dear.
He looked ahead without a word,
Then I knew he could not hear.
Oh, God, forgive me when I whine
I have two ears, the world is mine.

With feet to take me where I go
With eyes to see the sunsets glow
With ears to hear what I would know
I'm blessed indeed.
The world is mine.
Oh, God, forgive me if I whine.

Save your Strength

Many people lose energy by being in conflict with the world around them. The streets are dirty, the neighbors are noisy, people are discourteous, the internet is down, the cabs won't stop and a host of other major and minor annoyances make people react with distress. As one man said: "You can't count on anything any more."

Get your personal peace about such situations. As a start, remember one rule: It's not what happens, but what you think about it that gives misery or delight. Power is within. The power is in the person and not in the event. Of course, it would be nice if you could rely on things and people, but you can't. This fact is ordained so that you may learn self-reliance.

Detach from dependence on things and people – make them less important and you won't suffer when they fail. At the same time, know and claim that your good is from God, the universal source and support. Only your consciousness makes, orders and disposes things in your world.

Trust this and you will be less disturbed when things around you go wrong. React, of course, for reaction shows you are alive. But never react with despair. Then this funny thing happens. The freer and more independent you are, the more other people are attracted to you, the more they will cooperate with you and the more all things will work together for good.

Now I Am Secure

I am now living in divine mind, with my eternal good. Here I find a power and a peace that is unlimited. Infinite intelligence and wisdom are available to me at all times.
I cannot be without any good thing, at any time. God is a generous giver.
Abundance and security are always in my world. All the good things of life are mine to enjoy. I am a perfect spiritual being, guided by the one mind. Within me is a permanent and sustaining belief in the perfect rhythm and peace of life.

I enjoy complete freedom from fear, uncertainty or doubt, for God is my protection. The law of mind is always manifesting through me, in profusion and abundance and I know and accept it now.

The presence and power of spirit maintain right action and harmony in all my affairs. A unity of purpose blesses me now and I am divinely inspired to a richer expression of life. Love and understanding are ever present in my world, and I am strong in my place in infinite mind.

Slow me Down

Slow me down, Lord.
Ease the pounding of my heart by the
quieting of my mind. Steady my hurried
pace with a vision of the eternal each time.
Give me, amidst the confusion of my day, the
calmness of the everlasting hills.

Break the tension of my nerves and
muscles with the soothing music of the
singing streams that live in my memory.
Help me to know the magical restorative power
of sleep. Teach me the art of taking mini
vacations, of slowing down to look at a flower,
to chat with a friend, to pet a dog, to read a
few lines from a good book.

Remind me each day of the fable of the hare and the tortoise, that I may remember that the race is not always won by the swift; that there is more to life than increasing its speed.

Let me look upwards into the branches of the towering trees, and know that they grow tall because they grow slowly and well.

Slow me down, Lord, and inspire me to send my roots deep into the soil of life's enduring values, that I may grow toward the stars of my greater destiny.

The Road Not Taken
Robert Frost

Two roads diverged in a yellow wood
And sorry I could not travel both
And be one traveler, long I stood
And looked down one as far as I could
To where it bent in the undergrowth.

Then took the other, as just as fair,
And having perhaps the better claim,
Because it was grassy and wanted wear,
Though as for that, the passing there
Had worn them really about the same.

And both that morning equally lay
In leaves no step had trodden black.
Oh, I kept the first for another day!
Yet knowing how way leads on to way,
I doubted if I should ever come back.

I shall be telling this with a sigh
Somewhere ages and ages hence:
Two roads diverged in a wood, and I –
I took the one less traveled by,
And that has made all the difference.

About the Editor

Beverly Russell was born and educated in London, UK, and moved to the US in 1967, to pursue a career in publishing, as a journalist, book author and editor. New York City was her base for more than 30 years and it was there she met and studied with Elenore Wrench.

Beverly Russell has received numerous awards for her work, including a citation by Mayor Edward Koch, naming August 21, 1986 as Beverly Russell Day in New York City; a citation from the American Academy in Rome; honorary doctorate degrees in Fine Arts from Kendall College of Art & Design, Michigan, and Parsons School of Design, New York. She is the author of over a dozen books devoted to arts and spiritual matters.

The writings and verses in this collection were handed over to the editor more than
thirty years ago while Elenore Wrench was still alive.
Attributions have been made wherever they were known. Any omissions are purely accidental and will be corrected in future editions of the book if made known to the editor.

Personal Prayers

LaVergne, TN USA
08 November 2010
203859LV00001B